TO WIVES

EVEN the best of us will find that, at times, married life is a trial. However much we may endeavour to do the right thing, perplexities have an unfortunate way of looming up and clouding the horizon.

But here is a book full of sound advice. It should help you to sense dangers before they arise.

CONTENTS

I

THERE is not the slightest doubt about it: women can make or mar the marriage partnership more than men can. Therefore, if you find you are both drifting on the rocks, don't throw all the blame on your husband. Ask yourself fairly and squarely if you have done your best.

Remember that the happiness of the home depends in a great measure on you and your exertions. If the home is not a cheery place, don't expect your husband to spend more time in it than he can help. He will be kept late at the office and have pressing calls from mysterious friends; and then you will grumble that he is always out.

Don't be one of those wives who demand their husbands to do this or that for them. No man worthy of the name will be "bossed". On the other hand, don't be a tame kitten or a doormat, for husbands look down on spineless women. Steer a middle course and your husband will appreciate your wisdom.

Woman is more of an enigma than man. Therefore, if your husband has not understood your wishes, don't straight-way rate him as dull or heartless. It is quite likely that he cannot fathom you; and for that you are more to blame than he is.

Lots of women have an idea it is lowering to their dignity to be quite frank with their husbands. The happiest partnerships are those where husband and wife know each other through and through.

Don't expect any great measure of married happiness, if you are the kind of wife who sets out with the idea of not letting your husband dictate to you. That is only another way of saying that you want to dictate to him. If he is an average kind of husband there will be an explosion.

Don't carry on because your husband is not exactly what he was before you were married. Then, you only saw him in his leisure hours: now you have him on a work-a-day footing. And the two are not exactly the same.

It is not clever to run down your husband to friends and neighbours. You may think it makes you look big: but most people will agree with you at the moment, and go away and say you are a cat. Don't imagine for a moment that back-biting impresses anybody who matters.

Don't expect your husband to wait on you hand and foot when he is at home. If he likes doing it, let him. But you have no right to look for such attentions. Just remember that his half of the bargain is to bring home the money and yours is to run the home.

Talking of money, don't be the type of wife who wheedles every farthing she can get out of her husband. The family finances ought to be very carefully worked out and you should not take a penny more than your share.

Wives are usually better at saving than husbands, in spite of all the comic papers say. Therefore, if your husband makes a poor hand at the job, persuade him to let you be the banker for a trial period. But, if he agrees, don't forget that it is your business to accumulate something in the bank and not replenish your wardrobe.

Wives are really very lucky creatures, although many of them don't know it. They have a kingdom of their own, they can be their own mistress and they do not have to work with the clock, as many people have to. Therefore, don't grumble about the kicks when you have so many ha'pence.

It is a wife's duty to look her best. If you don't tidy yourself up, when you have done the bulk of the day's work, don't be surprised if your husband begins to compare you unfavourably with the typist at the office.

When your husband arrives home, give him a cheery welcome, so that he is glad to be back. It's a thing a man appreciates, especially when he is tired. But don't ply him with all the pointless tit-bits of news that you have heard during the day. Nor will he want to know that the maid broke a plate while washing-up. He will much prefer to look at you and admire the frock you made yourself.

Some wives manage their affairs so that they always have to be in some remote part of the house when their husbands pull the armchairs up to the fire and light their pipes. If you are a wife who does this, don't. Your husband is entitled to your company and he most likely misses it. He can grow accustomed to your absence and, in time, may prefer it. And, then, you will cry out that he is neglectful.

If your husband has a hobby that makes the place untidy, don't be too hard on him. It certainly is aggravating, at times, to find everything upside down. But look on the bright side of things, and thank your stars that he prefers to come home and be with you than to be sitting at the club and spending money.

Don't be all smiles when visitors come and then, when they have gone, be exactly the opposite. Your husband will be quick to notice the difference and he will draw his own conclusions.

Don't pose as a weak little thing that cannot go a journey unless your husband buys your ticket and puts you in the train. Wives who do this got out-of-date while Queen Victoria was alive. And a woman who still persists in being femininely frail has few admirers, to-day. Of course, if a wife asks her husband to come and see her off because she enjoys his company, that's quite another thing.

Are you a flirt? Because, if you are, there is trouble ahead for you, as sure as eggs are eggs. While the average husband likes his wife to be jolly and friendly with his men friends, there are very few who will tolerate flirting. Flirting is something that decent wives don't do.

Don't tell your husband that you can't be

bothered with business matters. It is your duty to get to understand the business of the home—such as paying the bills, the rates and so on. And, if you say you have no time for such things, he will begin to wonder whether you are really capable of handling the home purse.

Don't overlook the fact that the average husband likes being made a fuss of. If you do it honestly and don't gush about it, there is nothing he won't do for you. Of course, it has got to be genuine.

After all is said and done, husbands are not terribly difficult to manage. Certainly, they are not nearly as difficult as they imagine in their own hearts. If your husband is of the awkward class, you either picked a bad one or you don't know the elementary rules of "husband management". In either case, you must put some of the blame on yourself.

There is a saying which tells us to open our eyes wide before marriage, but to keep them half-shut afterwards. Yes, keep them half-shut afterwards is a very wise course to follow. All husbands have their little irritating ways and, if our eyes are half-shut, we don't see them, and, of course, they need not irritate us.

Don't neglect your husband's relations. We once knew a man who was rapidly tiring of his wife, and then his mother fell ill. The wife insisted that the mother should come to them to be cared for. The mother came and, in time, grew well again. The husband saw, as he had never seen before, the sterling qualities of his wife, and the crash was averted.

Don't run away with the idea that you will never lose your temper and that your husband will never lose his. You will both do it at times. The only thing is that you must not both lose it at the same time.

If you would like your husband to take you out, ask him to. Don't expect him to discover, in some mysterious way, that you want to go; and when he fails to find out, don't silently accuse him of being neglectful. You are simply being awkward, if you do.

The average husband would far rather buy his wife a new dress than get himself a fresh necktie. But, if your wardrobe is full of dresses and your husband's only tie is getting frayed at the edges, be reasonable and refuse the dress. Don't have it, and explain your reasons. Little actions of this kind are worth a great deal—more than all the dresses in Bond Street.

There is one great difference between a husband and a wife. If a husband starts a row, he will allow himself to say his mind pretty freely; but when he has said it, it is said and done with. The wife, on the other hand, may be more careful of what she says at the time, but she will rake it all up again at a later opportunity, and she will keep on doing it. This looks as though the man is more forgiving than the woman, which is after all something to his credit. Therefore, don't rake up old scores if you have any self-pride.

II

Do be careful that in your married partnership all your actions are those of kindliness. Remember that Shakespeare says:

> Kindness in women not their beauteous
> looks
> Shall win my love.

Don't forget that the golden rule for domestic happiness is the cultivation on both sides of absolute unselfishness. To attain the perfect union it should be the object of each to yield oftenest to the wishes of the other, provided such wishes are reasonable and right.

Do be careful not to expect everything of marriage at the outset. With the termination of the honeymoon comes a period of settling down, during which each has to learn the other's foibles. It may be that you will then find that your husband is not absolute perfection and consequently you may feel that you have been deceived. In such a case, ask yourself what qualities you possess that would entitle you to the possession of a perfect husband, and further, would you, on your part, be always able to live up to such perfection.

Don't expect your husband always to see things from your point of view. You will find it instructive and advisable sometimes to put yourself in his place for a change. Moreover a little healthy criticism always has its value.

Do remember never to scold or "tell off" your husband in front of others. It is embarrassing for them and lowering to his dignity. Wait until you are alone. It won't hurt by keeping, and probably by that time will have assumed its true proportions and will appear as a matter of little moment. Smile pleasantly, however annoyed you may feel.

Don't also go in for a "straight talk" when either of you is busy, tired, vexed or hungry. If you do, you will only go from bad to worse, especially if, in the case of a man, he is hungry. Wait until you are both rested and fed, and then it is highly probable that the cause of the trouble will be found to have disappeared.

Do, above everything, eliminate from your vocabulary that objectionable phrase "I told you so". To many men it is like a red rag to a bull, denoting as it does a certain amount of superiority rammed home. Further, don't remind your husband of past errors or mistakes. Rest content to let the dead past bury its dead.

Don't ever allow yourself to be angry at the same time as your husband. That will always result in matters becoming more serious. Also, never make a remark at the expense of each other, since the person attacked must either be silent or lose dignity by replying in kind.

To make any such remark is consequently mean.

Don't talk at one another either alone or in company. To do so in the last named case is to make everyone uncomfortable. Never allow yourself to drop into the vulgarity of shouting at your husband, the only occasions when it is permissible to do this is when the house is on fire, or someone is in grave danger.

Don't, when going out with your husband, make him late because some silly woman once declared that "it's good for a man to keep him waiting". Love and loyalty have never yet been born out of irritation.

Do try as far as possible to make your husband's interests your own. If, for example, he is interested in politics try and take an intelligent interest in them so that you can talk to him on more or less equal terms. The woman who fails to do this can hardly grumble if she is looked upon more as a doll than a partner.

Don't, on the other hand, allow him to over-ride your opinions if they are formed on adequate grounds. A woman who allows herself to descend into an echo will never win respect. The "obey" of the marriage service was never intended to suppress all individuality.

Do also insist that at all times you get from your husband the same respect that you would expect from any other man or that he would give to any other woman. Guard carefully against allowing him to become casual.

Don't sneer at the word "obey" in the marriage service and call it old fashioned. There is a great deal of truth in Tennyson's words that an obedient wife commands her husband.

Don't ever run the risk of proceeding in different directions. If there is any likelihood of this, call back to memory the happy hours of your early love.

Do realise that though husbands are sometimes a little tiresome in their requests nothing is troublesome that is done willingly.

Do be ever on guard that the words "don't care" never enter into the relationship of husband and wife. In the first place the use of them means that the parties are rapidly heading for disaster, and in the second that they are probably untrue, since only in extreme cases can the actions of one party be other than a matter of interest to the other.

Don't forget that a clever woman can always be the power behind the throne, and that she usually gets what she desires by making her husband believe that the idea which she puts forward was originally his own. It has been truly said that the road to success is filled with women pushing their husbands along.

Don't neglect the powerful weapon you possess in the shape of a little judicious flattery. Remember the lines:

Man flattering man, not always can prevail,
But woman flattering man can never fail.

Do try to realise that you can't expect your husband to spend all his evenings at home if you are too busy seeing about other things to sit down with him. See that he is cosily seated by the fire, has a pair of comfortable slippers, is wearing that old jacket that he loves so well, then take the chair at the other side of the fire and chat about everything that interests you both.

III

Don't get slovenly. The necessity for keeping smart doesn't conclude with the signing of the marriage register. Before marriage every girl naturally makes the most of her advantages and it is hardly fair to her husband if she ceases to do so once she becomes his wife. The woman who comes down to breakfast in a dingy old dressing-gown and bedroom slippers is going to suffer when compared with the smart little, well-turned out typist in her husband's office.

Don't forget that it is every married woman's duty to come down in the morning with a smile. It is the atmosphere of this early morning hour that largely colours the whole day, hence the advisability of your men folk going forth with the memory of a smile rather than a frown.

Do fight against any tendency to worry over little things that really don't matter. If your husband does not arrive home at the usual time, or by the usual train, it doesn't follow that he has been run over or has eloped with some other woman.

Don't become the slave of habit. It is doubtful if there is any person more annoying than the woman who cannot accompany her husband on some little excursion he has planned for them both because he has fixed it on the day for turning out the drawing-room.

Don't forget that a wife can always set the standard of behaviour for the home. If she allows laxities of dress or conversation at the table she will soon find that they become a fixed procedure.

Do take care not to become one of those persons who is always looking out for trouble or fancied insults. Everyone knows the type of person who is always imagining that she is going to be cut or ignored by one of her friends, and who generally replies to your greeting with: "I thought you weren't going to speak." Take it for granted that your friends are glad to see you—as they probably are.

Don't become a furniture wife. It's a very natural desire on your part to keep your drawing-room perfect, but don't fly into a rage if your husband goes in and generally upsets things. Scold laughingly, or better still head him off in some other direction. After all you must remember that it is his work or money that provides the room.

Do, if you have only two reception rooms, abolish the drawing-room. With only two, why reserve one for the unusual occasion? Make one room your dining-room, plainly furnished, and the other a lounge, common room or living-room where all the family can assemble and spend their time as they please.

Make it a room in which memory will at all times linger.

Don't allow yourself to grow excessively domestic. Evenings at home should be very happy ones, but owing to the weakness of human nature even the sweetest of things continued without variation will in time pall on one. Don't insist that your husband gives up all his bachelor interests and friends. A return to them occasionally will usually make him appreciate his home the more. On the other hand don't neglect to take your own share of outside interests. Don't allow yourself to grow dull. Keep up-to-date. Few husbands want only a housekeeper or a decorative head of the table. What they want is a companion who can talk with them on equal terms.

Don't forget that, while a little modernity is perhaps pleasing, an excess of it is usually nauseation. No lady ever smokes cigarettes in the streets. To do this is to label yourself at least ignorant or fast.

Don't also become one of the blood-red nail brigade. Most men dislike this attempt to improve on nature, especially as it is largely associated with the demi-monde.

Do endeavour at all times to look on the sunny side of things. This is a fortune in itself. Don't look on life through a smoked glass. Remember:

Life's a mirror; if we smile,
Smiles come back to greet us;
If we're frowning all the while
Frowns forever meet us.

Do not forget that it is necessary for women to be far more careful of their conduct than men. Unfortunately, appearances will often injure as much, if not more, than real crimes.

Don't grumble at this higher standard that is expected of a woman. After all it was woman herself who first set up a standard of manners, this, according to Rudyard Kipling, dating from the time when she was the first to choose to live in caves and to hang a horse skin before the door in order to obtain a certain amount of privacy.

Do learn to cultivate a spirit of humour. It has been well said that "the love of fun in human nature is a normal natural lubricant which oils life's machinery, makes it run smoothly and relieves the jar and grinding of the bearings which prematurely wear away life."

Don't ever allow yourself to get the reputation of being frivolous. It's one of the easiest reputations in the world to acquire and one of the most difficult to lose.

Don't forget the words of the old Roman sage written over 2,000 years ago but equally true to-day: "Levity of behaviour is the bane of all that is good and virtuous."

Do let it be your constant endeavour to keep yourself in every way toned up. Try at all times to maintain the freshness and sprightliness of the engagement days. Do a certain amount of dressing for the evening meal and make your men folk do the same.

Don't forget that there is nothing which destroys beauty so quickly as bad temper. This is a thing in which no woman can afford to indulge since it will soon make its evil mark upon even the most charming face.

Don't go around announcing that you are very sensitive. Perhaps you don't realise that this is an acknowledgment of weakness since it is founded on vanity, egotism and selfishness.

Do endeavour on all occasions to cultivate the sunny side of your nature. As you give out sunshine so will you imbibe it.

Don't allow yourself to waste your life on non-essentials. Don't upset the whole house by scolding or nagging over some little matter that won't matter a jot in a week's time Keep your energy for the things that really count.

Don't forget that our characters are very much influenced by the friends we make. Instinctively we absorb the qualities of those with whom we are brought daily into connection, hence the necessity of choosing only what is good.

Don't allow yourself to be one of those persons who can never make up their minds on any subject. Compel yourself to look at the matter from both sides, make your decision, and then stick to it.

IV

FOOD AND COOKING

Don't forget that very true remark that, while face powder may catch a man, baking powder is the stuff to hold him.

Do endeavour always to feed your husband and guests on food suitable to the occasion. No one is going to grow enthusiastic over cold mutton on a cold wintry day or over Irish stew on a boiling August mid-day.

Don't forget to serve all hot food really hot. This simple precaution will often cover a multitude of other culinary sins.

Do pay attention to your own meals when your husband is absent. Pastries and tea for lunch will soon ruin health, temper and digestion. Beware of the ever-flowing tea-pot. While being woman's comfort it is only too often her destruction.

Don't let breakfast be a scrap or hurried meal. See that everyone allows at least half an hour for it, and give as much care to its preparation as you would do to any other meal. Never forget that it is the one on which the best work of the day has to be done and that the human engine, like any other, won't function properly unless care has been given to the stoking.

Do try to aim at freshness and variety in the preparation of food. Don't get into a groove. Be adventurous and enterprising. Your steamed puddings may be excellent, but that is no reason why your husband or family should be fed solely on them. Is there any reason why you shouldn't sometimes give your husband a pleasant surprise with a French dish?

Don't labour under the idea that cold meat is always cold meat and can never appear in any other form. Exercise your ingenuity in bringing it forward in some new and attractive manner even if it means more work.

Don't forget that cooking is an art in which you cannot neglect trifles—but don't serve them on all and every occasion.

Do bear in mind that the old, old advice to "feed the brute" remains as true to-day as it was a thousand years ago. Aim at freshness and variety in what you provide. Let meals be well balanced and health-giving. The digestions of your husband and family lie largely in your hands and you cannot expect a happy and contented household if these are far from being what they ought to be. Truly did Sydney Smith write: "Old friendships are destroyed by toasted cheese, and hard salt meat has led to suicide."

Don't lose any opportunity of increasing your culinary knowledge. After all, meals form a very large part of human life and if you wish to reign as a popular Queen of the home you must also be prepared to act efficiently in the role of Minister of the Interior.

Don't get into the only too common habit of serving meals anyhow when no one is present but your husband and yourself. Dainty service raises a meal from a mere means of keeping one's self alive to a desirable and pleasurable ceremony.

Do endeavour to avoid all subjects of conversation of a gloomy or worrying nature until the meal is over. Worry has a great effect upon digestion, and if you do admit them you will probably find they have nullified your best efforts at turning out a nice meal. To get the best results every meal should be a time of pleasure and happiness. Never forget the couplet:

You'd be astonished really at the benefit it yields—
Simply mix a little merriment and laughter with your meals.

Do try and get a little originality with the Sunday evening meal. Your guests will rise up and call you blessed if you give them something other than the stereotyped cold meat, salad and trifle.

Do let your store cupboard be one of the places to which you give most attention. You never know when the unexpected guests are going to turn up and your motto must be always "Be prepared.

Don't forget that it is not now the thing to offer red wine with strong flavoured food or any accompanied by sauces containing acids.

Don't, if you are wealthy enough to have a cook, let her decide what you shall eat and in what form it shall be prepared. Your husband pays the bills and it is only fair that his tastes should be considered.

Don't feel aggrieved if your husband mentions with pleasure some dish that his mother used to make. Write and ask her for the recipe and then give him a surprise by producing it.

Do cultivate the old-fashioned custom of largely filling up your store cupboard with articles that you have made yourself. It may be just as cheap to buy your jam at the shop but it probably won't be made of such good materials and the family will certainly agree that the shop article doesn't taste half as good as yours.

V

DRESS AND TOILET

Do bear always in mind that refinement in dress is generally associated with refinement in manners.

Don't dress for other men or women, not even to outdo the latter, but dress for your husband. Do this with the same care that you did before you were married. If there is a particular dress that he likes, put it on occasionally even if it is out of fashion. Never forget that in matters of dress a man is usually conservative, and once he has settled he likes something that you wear he will go on preferring it even to the latest Paris creation.

Don't overdress for a restaurant or small dinner. A dinner dress is all that is necessary.

Do be careful, if going for a week-end in the country, not to let your wardrobe consist entirely of frills and furbelows. It may upset your husband if you can't visit some beauty spot on which he is keen, or accompany him on a long country walk, because your shoes are only suitable for pavements.

Don't, unless you have money to spare, go in for extremes in dress which more or less date themselves. If your dress allowance is limited go in for good material, well cut and tending to a uniform rather than an extreme style.

Don't make up on the dance floor or in any public place. The proper place for that is the dressing-room.

Don't laugh at your husband's ideas as regards dress, and don't suggest that men know nothing about such a subject. After all your main idea should be to wear something that he likes, and most men do have both good and original ideas on the subject. Remember that the leading dress designers are men, not women.

Don't forget that the best form of face massage is to be constantly smiling. Wrinkles cannot exist on a smiling face, while contentment has ever been known to be the fountain of youth.

Do remember that there is one rule of dress which apparently never changes and that is that it is not good form for a hostess to be dressed more richly than her guests. If in any doubt it is best to play for safety and err on the side of simplicity.

Don't forget to give some attention to your husband's wardrobe. Men are proverbially careless in this respect, and it is up to you to see that he turns out in such a way as to do you credit.

Do endeavour not to take your husband on a long and distinctly feminine shopping expedition. If you want his opinion on some particular point see to that first and then let him run off on his own business.

Don't be sarcastic or overbearing when your husband's ideas as regards what he should wear do not coincide with your own. If he wishes to wear a startling red and blue club tie with a brown lounge suit don't laugh him to scorn but persuade him gently into the right path.

Do not forget that among the things most dangerous to love are untidy hair, faded negligée, curlers and bedroom slippers at the breakfast table. Above everything try to make a good and appropriate beginning to the day.

Do not be induced to wear something that doesn't suit you because all the other women are wearing. You ought to know what best suits you and should stick to that.

VI

CHILDREN

Do always bear in mind that one of the first duties of a parent is so to train the children that they may always appreciate the beauty to be found in life. Above all make them realise the beauty of common things. This will open up for them a thousand avenues of enjoyment unnoticed by those not so trained.

Don't forget the very true saying that in dealing with children kind words are the music of the world.

Don't be a prohibition mother. Don't tell the children ten times what they must not do and only once what they may do. It is the natural impulse of a child to be always doing something fresh, it is his or her little advance into the world of adventure, and the wise parent will help rather than hinder natural influences. Don't let your little one be like the small fellow, who, when asked his name, replied: "Charlie Don't."

Don't grudge the many sacrifices you have to make during the years of child rearing. You are only giving to the next generation what your parents gave to you. Further, can there possibly be any higher mission in the world than the training of its future citizens?

Don't ever make the terrible mistake of meeting a tired husband at the door and, before he has had time to hang up his hat, pour out a long list of the children's delinquencies. Wait until he has rested and fed, and the probability is that by that time they won't look half so important.

Do all that you can for the children, but in caring for them still remember that you have a husband and that at times he requires a little attention.

Do remember that while possessing the most wonderful baby in the world it is not good form continually to call people's attention to the fact. It is quite natural for you to think that the world has never before produced such a marvel, but if you endeavour to impress that upon people you will probably be met with smiles or yawns.

Don't forget that discipline is not a matter for the school only but for the home. Family life has been well described as God's own method of training the young.

Don't ever let your children become importunate in their demands. If you do, and they find that importunity succeeds, they will expect more and more. Make them realise from a very early age that you mean what you say. It is fatal to allow whining or coaxing to alter your decision once it is made.

Don't monopolise to yourself the training of the children. Call your husband into your confidence and consult with him. While this will have the effect of making him realise his equal responsibility—a point that is often forgotten—it will also give you the benefit of a second opinion.

Do be ready at all times to make sacrifices for your children, but don't carry this too far. In the matter of dress, for example, be better equipped than your children so that they may look up and not down on you. Don't stint yourself to the extent of making your old dress do so that your son may have new flannels. By doing so you will very probably make him vain and selfish.

Don't give the small boy the same name as his father. Remember there will come a time when they may be "Old John" and "Young John".

Don't date a girl by her name. Jubilee may be a very nice name but the possessor of it won't thank you for giving it to her in thirty years' time.

Do, from their earliest years, teach the boys to pay every respect to women, not forgetting their sisters. The boy who is so brought up will find himself welcome and at ease in any class of society. Sternly repress that only too common idea among some boys that anything will do for the girls.

Don't repress children's conversation at the table but even encourage it. Never use that objectionable phrase "children should be seen and not heard" which has done so much to repress individuality. Don't, on the other hand, allow them to over-ride the conversation, and don't permit too much teasing or cheap chivvying.

Don't allow the children in any way to depose you from your position as Queen of the home. Insist upon the respect that is due to you. See that the boys open the door to you on every occasion.

Don't run to either extreme as regards the amount of the children's society that you allow to their father. Leave it at the point where he always requires a little more. Don't keep them unduly away from him in your desire that he should not be worried, and on the other hand don't allow them to be all over him at a time when he is tired and worried.

Do at all times impress upon the children that whatever family differences there may be these must be confined to the home circle and never carried into society. Family loyalty must always be the rule.

Don't be over anxious about the children and so grow old and faded before your time. Remember that you owe a duty also to both yourself and your husband. On the other hand don't be careless and leave them too much to others. Children of necessity mean sacrifice, and you should never be dressing to go out when for some good reason the little ones require your presence.

Don't find fault unless you are quite certain that a fault has been committed, and when it is necessary let it be brief and to the point. If you want to retain your children's love, never nag.

Do endeavour at all times, and especially when children are present, to be as pleasant at your own table as you would be if you were a guest at that of someone else.

Do try to make your children's surroundings all that they should be. We are all of us very much like whispering galleries, giving back only the echoes of what we have heard.

Don't ever let one of your children feel that you do not trust them. Such a thought will at once drive the child in the opposite direction to that which you desire. Advise, sympathise and let him or her see that you have full confidence; that there will be a striving to do what is right.

Do take the greatest care not to let your children in any way grow old before their time. Keep the serious side from them as long as you reasonably can so that they may have a chance to develop in the sunshine of life.

Don't fly into a temper if Daddy takes the small boy out for a walk looking a perfect little dream, but brings him back perfectly happy but more or less covered in mud. After all they've both probably had a good time and

have learned to know quite a good deal of each other in that short while.

Do bear always in mind that with children both parents have an object in life and, what is more, a sacred responsibility. With them you have something to work for, and if this is faithfully carried out, with its attendant sacrifices, it is bound to have an ennobling effect upon your character.

Don't forget your thanks for the great and wonderful gift of children. They may at times be troublesome, but would you for all the world can offer miss the feel of those little arms around your neck?

VII

DON'T waste hard earned money in the endeavour to keep up appearances. It is the height of foolishness to do things or buy articles that you cannot afford simply to impress your neighbours who probably, all the time, are only laughing at your efforts.

Do not be led into buying something that you do not want simply because it is cheap.

Do keep accounts. There certainly are times when to do this is somewhat of a trouble, but on the other hand your husband has a right to know how his money is being spent.

Don't neglect to pay your bills regularly. The person who settles at any odd time never knows how she stands, and sooner or later will probably find it necessary to go to her husband to help her out.

Don't rush into some lavish expenditure that you really cannot afford. Remember that pride has always cost more than hunger or thirst.

Do endeavour to settle your financial arrangements before marriage, or at any rate directly after. However small your joint income may be a certain proportion should be allotted to housekeeping, and a separate amount to yourself as a personal allowance to cover dress, recreation, etc. After all, even the servant gets her wages as well as her board, and there is nothing more humiliating for a wife than to have to ask her husband for the money for every little purchase she may make. Claim your separate allowance and see that you do not exceed it.

Don't say you are too busy if your husband wants to discuss finance. After all, it is a very important part of life, and every woman should know exactly her husband's position. As you are partners you ought to know how the bank balance stands just as much as your husband.

Do try always to be economical but don't let it develop into unnecessary pinching and saving. The tragedy of only too many people is that they deny themselves the legitimate pleasures of the moment to save for their old age, and when this is reached they are too old to get any pleasure out of their money.

Don't expect to begin where your parents left off. Remember that their standard of comfort is the result of many years of labour and that a little hardship and struggle at the outset won't hurt you but will make the easier time that comes later all the more pleasant.

Don't make the mistake of denying yourself too much in order to pile up money for the children. Give them a good education and a start in life and you have done your duty. Moreover, in the case of youth, money acquired without effort often goes very rapidly.

Don't spend up to the limit of your income and don't allow your husband to do so. Insist upon a fixed proportion being put aside for the "rainy day".

Don't allow the little capital thus obtained to be drawn upon except as an extreme measure. To draw out is easy, but to replace is an entirely different matter.

Don't practice your pet economies on other people. It is very laudable to endeavour to keep down your household expenses but it is scarcely diplomatic constantly to give your husband some article of food which he does not like in preference to one which he does appreciate simply because it is a halfpenny a pound cheaper.

Do be careful in money matters not to trade upon the love or the good nature of your husband. If he is generous to a fault it is the more up to you to see that your calls upon him are reasonable. Play your part fairly as a partner and take only your legitimate due.

If your husband's income falls in any way don't wait for him to suggest it but bring forward at once any methods by which you can economise in the housekeeping.

VIII

Do endeavour when introducing two of your guests to each other to start the conversation with some subject in which they will both be interested. It is hardly sufficient to introduce them; remark on the weather, and then leave them to themselves.

Don't invite guests who will clash. Select them as carefully as you would your menu. Don't commit such a faux pas as to invite to the same dinner party a husband and wife who have recently been divorced.

Don't make a fuss at the arrival of some unexpected visitor, especially if your husband brings home some old friend. It may be rough luck when you have nothing prepared, but remember that it always upsets a man if he joyfully brings home an old chum and then only gets a cold welcome.

Don't refuse to entertain because you can't do it on a champagne basis. With a little care and trouble it is possible to run the jolliest of little parties on claret cup.

Do remember, if you are anxious for your party to succeed, never to attempt anything beyond your resources. If you can't offer much then offer little, but let it be good. Better a plain dinner well cooked than an ambitious one badly done.

Don't omit when sending out invitations to consult your husband first. Let the suggestion that his relatives be invited come from you, not him. Take care to invite anyone whom he thinks will further his interests, and don't forget his old and bachelor friends.

Do be careful when entertaining to ask the right people at the right time. Don't ask the Vicar to supper on a Sunday evening after he has preached three sermons and taken a Sunday School and three christenings. It is probable that the one thing on earth that he desires is to go home to bed. Similarly don't ask the man who works till midnight on a Saturday to lunch on the Sunday. He would probably much rather spend the whole morning in bed.

Don't press your guests to try everything on the table. That may have been good manners a generation or two ago but now is the height of bad form. Also don't force them into indigestion by using that ridiculous phrase: "Why, you're eating nothing!"

Do take every care not to get into disagreement on any point with your husband when guests are present. Even more important take care to avoid bringing anyone else into the controversy. It is both embarrassing and unfair to a guest to put him into the position of having to take sides.

Don't treat your visitors to a long description of some recent family illness or, even worse, to an account of some operation. Don't talk about slimming and different kinds of diet. As far as possible keep the subject of your own children—however clever they may be—in the background. A refreshing feature of the present time is that even the once popular subject of servants and their misdoings is now rapidly losing ground.

Don't go to the door to show one lady out while there are any remaining guests. Ring for the maid to do it. In the event of any male members of the family being present it is their duty to escort the lady to the door, in which case the services of the maid are not necessary.

Do try to make as much fuss of your husband's friends as if they were your own.

Don't follow the one-time custom of letting your table "groan" under the weight of the viands. For a small dinner three courses are quite sufficient, and to provide more savours of ostentation.

Don't try to give your guests the things to which they are accustomed but rather the things to which they are unaccustomed. They will appreciate the change, and it is much better than giving them somewhat laboured imitations of their own style. You would not expect, nor would you desire, a French household to offer you roast beef.

Don't, when entertaining, keep the gramophone or wireless going all the time.It is certainly wearing to the nerves and destructive to the conversation and there are probably some of your guests who like a little of the latter.

Don't forget, when inviting a guest to stay with you, to state the definite period of time for which you are inviting. Don't leave them in the uncomfortable position of not knowing whether the stay is to be for a week-end or a longer period.

Do not omit, if your guest is a stranger to the neighbourhood, to give full information as to the best means of travel. If coming by train suggest an hour of arrival that will be convenient to yourself, giving an alternative one in case that is not suitable for the other party.

Do endeavour, if your house is in the country, to send some conveyance or go yourself to meet any friend who is coming by train. If sending a car notify your guest of the fact and give information as to how it can be recognised.

Do take care that every guest room is supplied with writing materials, a reading lamp and a few carefully selected books.

Do remember to notify your guest if you propose to offer any special form of amusement, such as tennis or boating, in order that they may come properly prepared.

Don't overdo your guests in the matter of entertaining. Many of them doubtless will only be too glad to have a quiet time by your fireside and will not thank you for rushing them off from one thing to another or taking them on a round of visits to people whom they are not likely to meet again. Try to find their wishes and then act accordingly.

Don't, on the other hand, rush to the opposite extreme and, having told your guest to make herself at home, leave her to do so. Don't forget that it's not always easy at once to make yourself at home in someone else's house or to become one of the family within the space of an hour or two. Find out your guest's likes and dislikes and don't take it for granted that they will be the same as yours.

Don't forget that the perfect hostess never gives the impression that the usual routine of the house has been altered for her guests.

Do take care that you provide something more interesting for callers who are kept waiting than family albums and old volumes of poetry. Such mental food is scarcely likely to put your visitor in the most cheerful frame of mind.

Do be careful that if one friend arrives while you are entertaining another, your reception of each is equally cordial. It is somewhat upsetting for the one who has been greeted with a simple "Good afternoon" to find the next comer welcomed with gushing enthusiasm.

Do not make the mistake of asking a departing guest to post letters or parcels for you, and above all don't ask them to carry back a book which they have lent you. Borrowed books should always be taken back personally or sent by post.

Don't commit the unpardonable sin of being still at your dressing table when your guests are assembling for a party. The awkward feeling this will give them will be greatly increased if two or three guests unknown to each other are waiting in the drawing-room at the same time.

Don't try to force on your neighbours some form of entertainment for which apparently they do not care. In a locality where bridge playing holds undisputed sway it is not of much use trying to introduce musical evenings. If you do want to bring in variety it must at least be something original.

IX

Don't have one style of conversation for home and another for abroad. Have even a higher ideal for the former, especially where there are children.

Don't, when talking to other women, boast of your husband's success, cleverness, generosity, etc. As in the first place he belongs to you you are guilty of the social sin of boosting your own, while in the second it is hardly kind to those of your audience who are not so happily situated.

Do sometimes bring back to memory the fact that before marriage you used frequently to speak to your husband with your eyes,

whereas since, you probably do it more with your tongue. Continue still to give the eyes an occasional chance.

Don't be too fond of rubbing in home truths. It may sometimes be necessary that they should be told, but it does not often happen that they need be re-told. In any case let them be told, not in a spirit of triumph or vindictiveness, but in one of tact, sympathy and gentleness.

Don't cultivate a habit of cynical and sarcastic criticism. While a little criticism is often helpful and bracing, if carried too far it tends to depress and may even deliver a knock-out blow.

Do endeavour always to give praise when praise is due, but let it be genuine and never fulsome. It has been well said that the garment of true praise is the best for wear since it never goes out of fashion.

Don't in your conversation be self-conscious or shy. Fix your mind on what you are going to say and not only will your nervousness disappear but your sentence will come easily and fluently.

Do let your talk of others always be as far as possible kindly. If you can't say anything much that is good of them try, at least, to say nothing bad.

Don't adopt the only too common habit of breaking in when someone else is speaking. In addition to being rude it shows that you are putting very little value on what they are saying.

Don't discuss your own personal affairs or those of anyone else, in general conversation. Your business is your own and should be kept to yourself, and that of other people is their own and should be left to them.

Don't be one of those persons with a grievance who airs it on every possible occasion. Such persons are always bores.

Do make it a rule never to discuss mutual friends with anyone. It is remarkable how words may be twisted and made to injure even though there has been no desire to hurt.

Do listen as well as talk. You would scarcely have the temerity to claim that your words are sufficiently valuable to entitle you to monopolise the conversation.

Don't pride yourself on the fact that you always speak as you feel. If you do it is rather a thing of which to be ashamed since you won't be long before you upset someone. Tact in speech will succeed where directness of utterance only angers and throws into opposition.

Do take care that your language is at all times good but that you are at the same time concise. Don't repeat yourself. Take for your motto the epitaph on the woman in the Wesleyan Chapel, Wakefield:

Her manners mild, her temper such!
Her language good, and not too much.

Don't be one of those persons who only listen in order to put in what they consider is a brilliant comment. This is not the type of people who ever become welcome guests.

Don't forget that it is bad form to bring into any discussion such unpleasant topics as operations, diseases and particularly revolting crimes. Further, don't introduce family matters unless only members of the family are present.

Do refrain from laying down your likes and dislikes too emphatically when talking to mere acquaintances. Unless you know your ground pretty well your wholesale condemnation of something of which the other person approves is akin to telling him that his taste is abominable.

Don't ever greet an acquaintance at a party with the remark: "How did you come to be here?" Although you may not mean it so, it implies that you are surprised that they should be so honoured as to be allowed to be present at any place that you may see fit to honour.

Do take care in any conversation in a public place never to pitch your voice louder than necessary for your own party to hear. A neglect of this elementary precaution has often led to some awkward incidents.

X

OUT AND ABOUT

Don't drop out of society entirely when you get married. No woman can hope to keep up-to-date if she never exchanges opinions with others nor sees their ways.

Do remember however that such going out should be in moderation. Was it not St. Paul who gave the palm to the women who were stayers and workers at home? Find the happy medium which allows you to do your duty to yourself and your home, and then stick to it.

Don't omit when going out with your husband for the evening to be ready on time. Nothing irritates a man more than to be kept kicking his heels while his wife finishes dressing, and then for the two of them to arrive late.

Don't call attention to yourself in any public place by loud laughter, shrill conversation, or any eccentricity in dress or manner. These are among the things that are simply not done.

Do not call on your friends without previous invitation if you have any reason to believe that other guests may be present. If you do happen to call, and find such present, you should make your stay as brief as possible.

Don't, when being driven in a car, take upon yourself to help the driver to drive. Your suggestions will very likely only upset him and may lead to a serious accident. Leave him to do his job and don't interfere.

Don't, when going by taxi, stand at the side of your escort while he settles with the driver. Move on to the hall or the street door and wait for him there.

Don't expect any other lady with whom you are walking to introduce you to any of her friends she may meet. If she stops to speak to them do not stop also, unless requested by her to do so, but walk slowly on leaving her to catch you up.

Don't forget that if following a waiter to a table a lady should precede her male escort, but if a table has to be sought for by the escort then he should lead the way.

Do endeavour, when going to the theatre, to get to your seat five minutes before the advertised time for the curtain to go up. This will probably obviate the necessity for your upsetting other people in getting to your seat and will also give you time to look round.

Don't forget that your escort precedes you to your seat in the theatre, but on reaching the end of the row stands aside and allows you to go first.

Do be careful when going to stay with friends to acquaint them with the hour of your arrival. Also early in your stay announce the time of your departure, and don't alter it however much you may be pressed to do so. There are hostesses who, out of a mistaken sense of politeness, press all their guests to stay longer but really hope all the time they will not.

Don't, if driving a car, think that the rules of the road were only made for other people. Don't drive so as to raise clouds of dust. Don't drive near the pavement on a wet day so as to splash pedestrians. Don't sound your horn too freely, and don't let it be of the extra noisy variety.

Don't forget to send your letter of thanks to friends with whom you have stayed by as early a post as possible. To paraphrase a well-known saying: "She thanks twice who thanks quickly."

Don't, when staying at a boarding house, discuss its shortcomings with other guests, or, what is even worse, discuss one guest with another. In the former case your obvious line of action is to complain to the management and, if it isn't of sufficient importance for that, it isn't worth bothering about.

Do make every effort to be on time when invited to a card party. Tables cannot be made up until you have arrived, and to keep a whole party waiting is a social crime of the first magnitude.

Don't put off the taking of reasonable and legitimate enjoyment too long on the ground that you must wait until you have more leisure and more money. If this is carried too far there is grave danger that when the time comes that you do allow yourself a little pleasure you will find that you have got into a rut and that the capacity for enjoyment has gone.

Don't accept seats for the theatre at someone else's expense and then pull the play to pieces, giving your host the impression that you look upon the evening as wasted. Try and find some aspects of the play that you can praise. Remember there is nothing more disheartening than to set out with the idea of giving people pleasure and then discover that they have been bored.

Do make an effort to go out sometimes with your husband and don't always say that you can't leave the children. Make a special effort now and again to get someone to take over your duties and give your husband your company.

Do not feel that it is always necessary to take a lot of luggage when away from home. Learn the pleasure of travelling light and of, to some extent, roughing it. You will get far more fun than if you stayed at some fashionable hotel.

XI

HEALTH

DON'T adopt the "sofa disease". Beware lest you become one of those people to whom a lounge or sofa is almost a curse, since it is such a temptation to lie down and succumb to some trifling ailment or fancied illness.

Don't get into the habit of not feeling well, but brace up and do something exciting, preferably out of doors. Don't weaken your bodily powers of resistance to disease by a mental surrender without a show of fight.

Don't forget that it's quite possible to attract illness to oneself by constantly thinking about it. To think healthy thoughts is to do healthy acts and to attract health. To think diseased thoughts is to give way and to attract disease.

Do remember that a dragging feeling, loss of self control, constant headaches, a tendency to have to force yourself to work which was formerly a delight, are all Nature's warnings

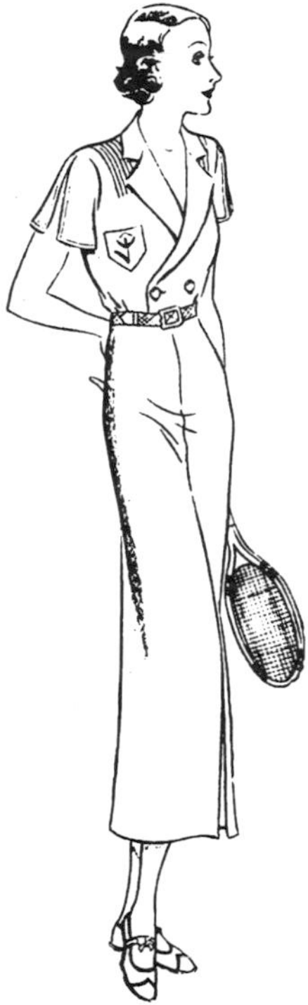

that you require a rest or change, and as such they must not be ignored.

Don't forget that one of the best doctors in the world is Mother Earth. The trouble is with most of us that we have become too artificial and do not realise that we should gain in health, strength, and efficiency if at least, for a time, we went back to a simpler life. Try the simple, healing power of the countryside rather than the nerve-racking amusements of the fashionable seaside resort.

Do realise at all times that the foundation of good health lies in leading a regular life. There must be sufficient sleep, sufficient exercise in the open air, sufficient change and recreation, and regularity and system in the mode of life.

Do take care to have some interests outside the daily routine of household duties. Monotony and lack of mental occupation are among the foremost of age-producers. Don't forget the old Grecian saying that the secret of eternal youth was to be always learning something new.

Don't, if at any time you have been unfortunate enough to have an operation, dwell on it. Put it out of your memory, and above all don't talk about it unless you wish to bore other people and increase your own weakness.

Don't be one of those people who "enjoy poor health" and whose conversation might well be described as an organ recital. Polite people may listen to you but they won't seek your company.

Do try to bear ever in mind that ill-health, and by this is meant not imaginary but real ill-health, doesn't knock you out of the battle of life. Think of the number of people who in spite of great bodily suffering have achieved great things—Robert Louis Stevenson, Mrs. Elizabeth Barrett Browning, Charles Darwin and a host of others. Think of some invalids you know who, in spite of their disabilities, are the sunshine of the home.

Don't think that the path to good health lies in the constant taking of patent medicines.

Search rather for it in the direction of regular outdoor exercise, contentment and moderation in all things.

Don't expect good health by leading a sedentary life for thirty days in the month and then cramming the thirty-first with violent exercise. That is more likely to lead to a physical and nervous breakdown. In the matter of exercise be as far as possible regular and never go on after you are tired.

XII

GENERAL

DON'T forget that while the rôle of wife is the hardest and most exacting in the world it is still the most popular and with care can be made the happiest.

Do try not to fall into the common error of grumbling at the monotony of housework. Learn to find happiness in doing it well. A good laugh once a day will have the effect of making it seem much easier.

Do not forget in all your dealings with husband or children that the mightiest force in the world always has been, and always will be, the silent power of love.

Do bear always in mind in everything that you undertake that a good beginning' is half the battle.

Don't forget, when up against the rough things of life, to look about and take them by the smooth handle.

Don't chide servants in the presence of strangers. It's not fair on the servants to show up their faults to others, and it's decidedly embarrassing for the stranger.

Do remember that if you want to get the best out of life, you must be both tolerant and broad-minded. This entails overlooking a good many things with which perhaps you do not agree.

Don't burden the ship of life with useless cargo. Throw over everything which does not help to make the voyage more pleasant.

Don't fall into the error of attempting to run your own life, and that of everyone around you, according to programme. The result will probably be misery for all who come in contact with you.

Don't grieve over what might have been, but make the best of what is. Life is too short to spend it in repining. Learn from your past errors how to conduct yourself in the future.

Don't forget that marriage, like government, must be a series of compromises. Don't run away with the idea that this only applies to your husband but be prepared also to make yours.

Do try at all times to be courteous to everyone you meet. Remember the words of Bovee, "the small courtesies sweeten life; the greater ennoble it."

Do endeavour to live up to what is expected of you. It was once said that a wife is a gift bestowed upon a man to reconcile him to the loss of Paradise, but in the case of some women it is rather a case of preparing him for the tortures of a lower world.

Do let your ideals be high. Unless they are this and your purpose a lofty one, life will be far from being a success.

Do try to make your daily tasks an art rather than a labour. Such an endeavour will make the dull routine no longer a drudgery but something that is a real pleasure, and at the same time will give the home an atmosphere of refinement.

Don't think when you are thirty that forty-five is old age. It is a well-known fact that we are what we think, and to consider forty-five to be ancient will make us so by the time we arrive at that point. Be always as young as you feel, and keep young by associating with youth and sharing their plans, hopes and joys. On the other hand don't go too far and become kittenish.

Don't forget the little family anniversaries and especially that of your wedding. Keep them up however inexpensively. They are wonderful factors in drawing you together year by year and driving away the troubles of to-day in the golden memories of the past.

Don't fail to laugh at your husband's jokes. Even if they are poor bring out a smile for

them or, otherwise, if you fail him, he will feel properly crushed.

Don't forget that all domestic tasks can be carried out in one of two ways, either in the spirit of an artist or in that of an artisan. To be really happy in your work you must of necessity adopt the former.

Don't fall into the modern error of assuming that all the ideas held by your own or your husband's parents must be old-fashioned and out-of-date. Many of them have stood the test of time very well and in matters of behaviour, at any rate, are superior to those in vogue to-day.

Don't crowd your house with a lot of unnecessary silver and stuff that wants continual cleaning. This takes up a lot of time that might more profitably be spent with the children or in healthy outdoor recreation.

Do let one of your first duties as a married woman be to get some instruction on how to deal with the little accidents that so frequently occur in households. Learn also how to put on a bandage correctly. You will be very lucky if you don't require this knowledge sooner or later, and you will never forgive yourself if, when the occasion arises, you don't know how to act.

Don't be too stand-offish with your neighbours and pride yourself that you never bother with them. There comes a time in the life of everyone when we are only too glad of a little help and sympathy and we can scarcely expect it from those we have hitherto ignored.

This edition first published in 2008 by the Bodleian Library,
Broad Street, Oxford OX1 3BG
www.bodleianbookshop.co.uk
Reprinted 2008 (twice), 2009, 2010 (twice), 2011 (twice),
2012 (twice)

ISBN: 978 1 85124 381 5

This edition © Bodleian Library, University of Oxford, 2008
Originally published as *Do's and Don'ts for Wives*, by
Universal Publications Ltd in 1936.
Images adapted from illustrations in Army and Navy
catalogues from 1933 and 1934 taken from the John Johnson
Collection in the Bodleian Library, University of Oxford;
Women's Clothes and Millinery 8 (24) and (25) respectively.

Cover design by Dot Little
Internal design by JCS Publishing Services,
www.jcs-publishing.co.uk
Printed and bound in China by C&C Offset Printing Co. Ltd.

British Library Catalogue in Publishing Data
A CIP record of this publication is available from the British
Library

How to be a

Good
Wife

Bodleian Library
UNIVERSITY OF OXFORD